Unplugged: Workplace to Worldplace

Simone Fenton-Jarvis

Presentation by *BookLeaf Publishing*

Web: www.bookleafpub.com

E-mail: info@bookleafpub.com

ISBN:9789358369892

First edition 2024

ACKNOWLEDGEMENT

To anyone who has ever questioned whether they are more than their job titles, this book is a tribute to you. The pursuit of a richer, fuller life beyond the workplace has been the driving force behind my thoughts and reflections on these pages.

Thank you all for being a part of this journey. "Unplugged: Workplace to Worldplace".

PREFACE

Hello!

Welcome to "Unplugged: Workplace to Worldplace."

I'm thrilled to share with you a journey that transcends the boundaries of the workplace and explores my world beyond work hours.

The driving force behind this book is a profound realisation: I am more than my job. In a professional capacity, I've had the privilege of delving deep into the intricacies of culture and employee experience. But, this book is not about the boardroom or corporate strategies. It's about the moments when I unplug from work, allowing my passions and musings to come to life.

In the following chapters, you'll accompany me on a voyage where I explore topics close to my heart. From the endearing antics of badgers and border terriers to the contemplation of introversion in a world that often celebrates extroversion, from concerns about the pressing issue of climate change to the ever-evolving journey of adulting, each page reflects a facet of my world.

My aim in sharing these thoughts and experiences is to inspire you to discover what makes you tick in a world where work can easily take over. I believe that work should be a part of life, not the entirety of it. Through my words, I hope to convey the beauty of embracing the world in all its diversity and to remind us all that we are indeed more than our job titles.

So, I invite you to join me on this journey from the workplace to the worldplace - a journey that celebrates the truth that we are, in fact, more than our jobs.

Be a good human,
Simone.

Beyond the Title

In a city where dreams take flight,
I cherish my job with all my might.
A workplace consultant throughout the day,
Yet beyond my title, there's more to convey.

I'm not just a role, not just a career,
I've got other passions, abundantly clear.
Badgers and terriers, steal my heart,
Friends, coffee and a Bakewell tart.

Football and ice hockey, a love for a board
game,
It's the stadium's roar and the rink's frozen
frame.
Music that moves, travels that inspire,
In this grand journey, they light my fire.

In change management, I find my stride,
Employee experience, on this journey I ride.
But remember, I'm human, I've got my own
song,
A symphony of passions, where I truly belong.

So, when the day's work is put on the shelf,
I find joy in reading, and capturing life's wealth.
Playing FIFA, scoring goals with delight,

Taking photographs, freezing moments in time
so bright.

I'm more than my job, as years unfold,
Come closer, let's connect, there's stories untold.
As connections deepen, we all grow,
Through life's twists and turns, we radiantly
glow.

More than my job, a heart and mind whole,
Together, navigating the world as we stroll.

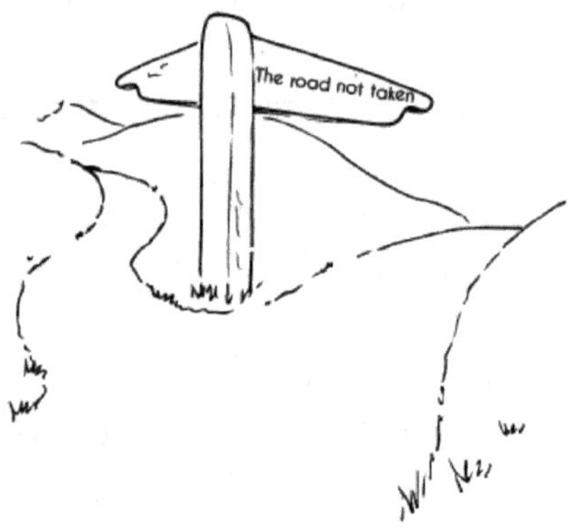

Paws for Contemplation

Badger, badger by the garden gate,
Sniffing the air as I stand and wait.
In the shadow of policies so extreme,
A badger at the gate, a lovely scene.

Amidst the controversy it lingers there,
Misunderstood, in a world where compassion is
rare.
Badger, badger you shine so bright,
Foraging and snuffling under the soft moonlight.

Innocent eyes, filled with trepidation,
Caught in a storm of contentious narration.
As the badger cull looms, a divisive debate,
The beautiful creature awaits its uncertain fate.

A badger at the gate, praying for its life,
As I take photos to show to my wife.
In the quiet of night, it stands so still,
A living creature subject to human will.

In the face of this challenge, we must
contemplate,
The sniffing, innocent badger at the garden gate.

Pages of Purpose

In the world of business, where knowledge is
gold,
I embarked on a journey, stories to unfold.
With data and facts, I began to compose,
A non-fiction book where wisdom steadily
flows.

Each chapter a lesson, a guide to success,
In the corporate landscape, aiming to impress.
From strategy to leadership, the insights clear,
A roadmap to humanness, year after year.

Through interviews and research, tools at hand,
Crafting solutions, helping businesses meet
demand.
In this non-fiction world, where theories took
flight,
I shared practical wisdom, to ignite a light.

The manuscript's done, a labour complete,
Infusing human touch in every workplace seat.
For leaders and learners, a guide they can't overlook,
In the pages, I penned, "The Human-Centric Workplace" book.

The Art of Alignment

In the rush of the workplace, a constant race,
I sought a different rhythm, a quieter space.
To do less, not from laziness, but with intent,
A shift in perspective, to be more content.

In the stillness, I found a mindful retreat,
The value of pausing is truly sweet.
For in doing less, I found room to breathe,
A respite from chaos, a moment to seethe.

To prioritise tasks, with wisdom and care,
Not overwhelmed by the daily work's glare.
With efficiency and focus, I charted my way,
Balancing work and life, come what may.

In doing less, I discovered the art,
Of finding fulfilment and peace at heart.

Timeless Ties

Long friendships, like roots deep in the earth,
A bond that grows, of infinite worth.
Through life's twists and turns, they persist,
In the chapters of time, they always exist.

Shared laughter, and tears, joys, and strife,
These friendships have woven the threads of
life.
They weather the storms, stand strong and true,
A testament to the love between me and you.

With memories spanning years, like a timeless
song,
These friendships endure, unwavering and
strong.
From childhood innocence to the wisdom of age,
Long friendships are a treasure, a heartwarming
stage.

In life's journey, they're the compass that's right,
Guiding us through darkness, as day turns to
night.
For in the embrace of these friendships, we find,
A love that grows deeper, forever entwined.

A Labyrinth

In the corridors of my restless mind,
Overthinking, a habit hard to unwind.
A tangled web of thoughts, they swirl and spin,
A ceaseless dance that never wears thin.

From past regrets to future's haze,
Overthinking keeps me in a silly maze.
Each decision, analysed and weighed,
In this mental chaos, I'm oft dismayed.

What if's and maybe's, prevent my peace,
The cycles that just never cease,
In the quest for answers, I lose my way,
In overthinking's grip, I often stay.

But in moments of clarity, I find release,
A chance to let go and find that peace.
For life's complexities, I can't always unwind,
But in simple moments, serenity I find.

For the Love of the Game

A long-suffering Oldham fan, that's me,
Through ups and downs, for all to see.
From legends of old, to new stars on the rise,
In their quest for glory, we see the fire in their
eyes.

The Latics, they've had their trials and
tribulations,
But my loyalty knows no reservations.
The highs and the lows, the victories and strife,
In our hearts, Oldham Athletic, the love of our
life.

Though trophies may be few and far between,
In the stands, I cheer, with a heart so keen.
The cheers and groans, the rollercoaster ride,
In this football journey, I stand with pride.

So, here's to the Latics, with passion we cheer,
Through every challenge, through every year.
As an Oldham Athletic fan, it's a lifelong
devotion,
In this football journey, our hearts are in motion.

In the Chair

In therapy's gentle space, we find our voice,
A sanctuary where hearts can make their choice.
With empathy flowing, without judgment or
haste,
We soften, and finally find our place.

Through the ups and downs, the joys and tears,
Talking eases the deepest fears.
In the comforting presence, learning to unbind,
The layers of the soul, the tangles of the mind.

Through tears and laughter, we navigate,
The maze of the mind, of both early and late.
A relationship forged in trust and in care,
With a therapist's guidance, we learn to repair.

In words unspoken, emotions untold,
Therapy's embrace is a hand to hold.
A space for self-discovery, profound and real,
Where emotions are valid, where we can heal.

In the chair, the soul finds reprieve,
A chance to talk, reflect and believe.
The therapist's wisdom, a guiding light,
In the darkest corners, they help us find sight.

To unravel thoughts, to release the past,
In therapy's refuge, we're free at last.
In this collaborative voyage, we learn to cope,
Discovering strength and resilience, and a
sprinkle of hope.

The Voyage

To be human is to dance with contradictions,
A blend of courage and life's afflictions.
With hearts that can break and spirits that mend,
In our human journey, we'll find the strength to
ascend.

We laugh and we cry, we love and we fear,
In our diverse emotions, our humanity is clear.
We build bridges and bonds, reaching out with a
hand,
Connection and empathy are what make us
grand.

In our quest for knowledge, we strive to explore,
The mysteries of existence, the tales never bore.
Yet, in the grand scheme, we're a fleeting breath,
A moment in time, between birth and death.

Our stories are unique, like stars in the night,
In the vast cosmos of humanity's light.
To be human is to live, to learn, to grow,
In this journey, let humanity show.

With dreams and hopes that inspire,
In the essence of being human, we all conspire.
To make the world better, to leave our own trace,
The human adventure, a marvellous race.

Tea, Rain and Brexit Pain

In the land of Britannia, where hearts once beat
strong,
A nation divided, where things went wrong.
Brexit's stormy seas, a tumultuous ride,
Many in disarray, on either side.

Tory Britain's policies, a cruel divide,
Inequality and cuts, they couldn't hide.
Austerity's heavy hand, squeezing tight,
With many struggling, day and night.

But in the midst of turmoil, voices scream,
Disappointed, angry, it feels like a bad dream.
In unity and protest, we find the might,
To confront the damage, to set things right.

For change is a constant, as time rolls on,
In the face of adversity, some grow strong.
Theresa May danced through fields of wheat,
While Boris Johnson's hair defied gravity's feat.

Brexit debates, oh, what a chaotic mess,
From "Strong and Stable" to "Get Brexit Done,"
no less.
Through it all, the British spirit stays,
With satire and wit, in these challenging days.

So, hold that cuppa high and mind the gap, if you please,
With wellies and brollies, until the raindrops ease.
In this land of laughter, where humour's our dearest friend,
Through turmoil and chaos, we'll laugh 'til the end!

For the Love of Dog

In the realm of true crime, I've often seen,
The complexities of human nature on the screen.
But there's a difference that I can't deny,
Watching dogs suffer, makes me cry.

For people's stories, I can sometimes detach,
Analysing the facts, and emotions to match.
But when it's about dogs, so innocent and pure,
Their pain and suffering, it's hard to endure.

Their loyalty and love, unwavering and strong,
Innocence in their eyes, where they belong.
So, yes, it's true, it's easier to bear,
The mysteries of people, with a curious stare.

But when it comes to dogs, our furry friends,
Their stories of hardship, my heart deeply rends.
In this world of true crime, where tales reside,
It's the pain of dogs, that I find hard to hide.

Sibling Bonds

In Manchester's embrace, childhood's sweet
reign,
With a brother by your side, a bond not
mundane.
10p mixes in hand, a sugary delight,
Warm sausage rolls, a messy bite.

Keenan and Kel on the screen, you'd eagerly
view,
Laughter echoed through the room, bonding like
glue.
Your Parents are Aliens, Hey Arnold and Worst
Witch,
Life was simple before it became a b*tch.

Through the lens of nostalgia, these memories
bloom,
A bond with your brother, like a well-woven
loom.
Childhood's treasures, simple and so dear,
In Manchester's embrace, you hold them near.

The busyness of life takes us far and wide,
Passing like ships, moving with the tide,

With family events, each one a lively show,
My heart remains humble as the memories glow.

Conference Confessions

In the midst of the conference's grand debut,
As an introvert, I share a unique view.
While extroverts network with zest and cheer,
I'm in the corner with coffee and my fear.

Small talk and handshakes, all quite draining,
Plotting escape routes, my introvert's training.
I greet selfie requests with a smile and grace,
Then seek solitude, in my own cosy space.

Amidst the conference's hum, in my introvert's
realm,
Sipping coffee, away from the noisy overwhelm.
While others converse, in their voices entwined,
I wander through thoughts in the haven of my
mind.

Don't mistake my reticence for disinterest,
please,
In my thoughts, I'm weaving ideas with ease.
For this introvert, humour is the expertise,
In subtle chuckles, sweet release.

I'm grateful for connections, for liking people I
meet,
But recharging in solitude is my ultimate treat.
I may not be the loudest, the star of the show,
But in my own way, I'm ready to glow.

Smashing Avocados, and Home Ownership Dreams

In the world of millennials, we face a strife,
An existential crisis, about avocado life.
Oh, the fruit so green, so creamy, so grand,
We believe it's the key to adulthood's land!

But wait, what's this? Prices have soared,
Avocado toast, we can't afford!
Our dreams of homeownership slowly fade,
As avocados steal our future's shade.

They dub us hipsters, with brunch on display,
Avo-toast in hand, we'll find our way.
The crisis of our generation, so it seems,
Is smashed avo in our wildest dreams!

And in this political climate, where house prices
climb,
We ponder our choices during avocado time.
Vintage clothes, vegetarianism, with the planet
in sight,
Through our values, we're living life just right.

But, don't forget the browning, oh-so-profound,
Avocado timing, a challenge renowned.
It's all about that moment, when it's ripe and just
right,
One second too late, it's brown at first sight!

In the Garden

In Sheffield's green embrace, I make my stand,
A happy human with dirt-covered hands.
Beneath the open sky, my garden's my domain,
Where life unfolds in sunshine and rain.

The soil, my canvas, fertile and deep,
A world of secrets it's eager to keep.
With every bud, I feel my spirits rise,
Nature's beauty unfolds before my eyes.

In the garden's hush, my peace I seize,
Worries and stresses gently ease.
With each weed pulled and every bloom,
I create a sanctuary and silence the doom.

Here's to the garden where life's burdens take
flight,

With a robin's embrace, my heart feels just right.
Among leaves and petals, stories are spun,
In this green haven, my soul finds its sun.

Navigating from Playing to Paying

In the eyes of youth, adulthood gleams,
A realm of hopes, or so it seems.
Freedom's beacon, a golden prize,
Where the world's a canvas, beneath open skies.

We yearn for the day when we're tall and free,
No bedtime rules, just endless spree.
But as years drift by, our dreams slowly unwrap,
We learn that adulthood's a complex trap.

Responsibilities pile, a weighty load,
Bills, work, decisions along life's road.
The carefree days of youth seem so far,
As grown-up life reveals its authentic avatar.

Adulthood's a mix of joy and despair,
Moments of wonder, moments that wear.
We chase dreams and confront challenges
galore,
In this intricate journey, we find what's in store.

So, to the little one with aspirations vast,
Remember, adulthood's not a trap that'll last.
It's a story, a path to embrace and engage,

In life's remarkable book, we all have our own
page.

Embrace the passage, through the highs and the
lows,
As an adult, you'll thrive, in spite of the throes.
Though it's not what you'd pictured as a tot,
Adulthood's an adventure, let's cherish the lot.

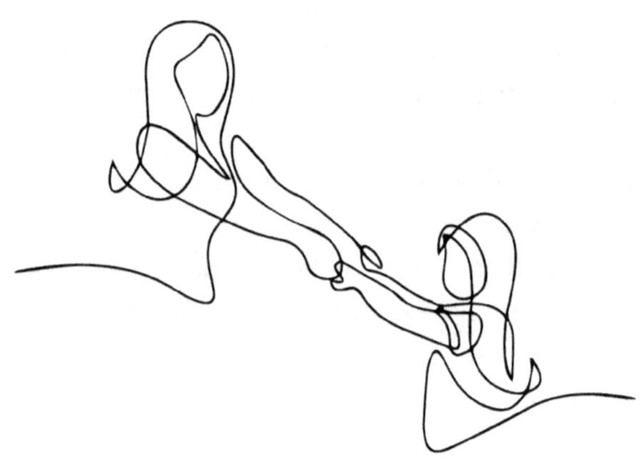

There's always hope

When things go wrong, and they usually will,
When every road feels like treacle, as you
plough up hill.
When the world feels dark and full of gloom,
When you watch the news and feel the
impending doom.
When you go to bed,
And wake still full of dread.
When you wish for more,
And from the empty jug you try to pour.

Relax, breathe, stay still,
And keep fighting your human will.
Yes, yes it could be worse,
Yes, yes the Tories have raided the public purse.
But there is hope,
There is always hope.

Better Together

In the comfort of our cherished home, you see,
Simple moments with you, set my spirit free.
Nowhere I'd rather be, you and me,
On the sofa, with the dog, watching crap TV.

We've explored countries, countless steps we've taken,
But it's in these still moments, our love's awakened.
Stacking the dishwasher, side by side,
Dancing in the kitchen, our love can't hide.

Through the aisles of the store I'd roam,
Doing the food shop, you'd plea to go home.
Your laughter always lightens the load,
And I adore the way we speak in code.

Changing the bed sheets, it's a gesture so true,
Through these simple acts, I cherish you.
From the ordinary to the extraordinary, we'll climb,
Our love grows through space and time.

In these moments, through life we weave,
Simple, yet strong, in what we believe.
Lions on ice and calls from your mum,

Our first date flew, now we're made out of glue.

Life is worth it, with you by my side,
Through sickness and in health, always my
guide.

Wanderlust

We queue in line and board the flight,
Our excitement soon shines bright.
We zoom to another place,
Somewhere I only know your face.

We chase the views or a city's embrace,
Discovering corners, in each new place.
Sampling flavours, cultures, and sound,
In this adventure, our hearts are bound.

We roam the street.
With our aching feet.
Looking up, looking around,
Our wanderlust is found.

Memories Simmered with Love

When I learned my Nanna had passed,
Grief struck me hard, a shadow cast.
Like a knife in my heart, I felt so undone,
The weight of the world, more than a tonne.

Her gentle smile, kind eyes and comforting
embrace,
Now memories etched in time and space.
Tears welled up as the news came to light,
With vodka, I sought solace deep into the night.

Grief like tides, has its ebb and flow,
I was told, 'In time you'll heal you know'.
Though she's not here, her love remains,
In the stories we share, in the love that sustains.

And oh, her soup. A warming delight.
On a cold winter's evening, a comforting sight.
In her kitchen, a pot simmered with care,
Her recipe of love, we continue to share.

Through the sadness, I find my way,
Honouring her memory every day.
In the depths of love, we'll always confide,
As I move forward with her love as my guide.

There's no Planet B

A familiar voice tells us the world's ice is in
plight,
For our arctic animals, there's not much light.
It's time to act, things are dire,
There's no time for tact, the world is on fire.

Burying our heads in the sand,
As fires spread across the Aussie land.
There's plastic in our seas,
There's no magic box, no magic keys.

We plant more trees,
We say 'what about the bees'
We need to reduce our waste,
Stop buying all the sh*t in haste

We need to reduce our carbon footprint,

Recycling bottles don't make a dint.
We need to change how we live,
A bigger damn we need to give.

As the Seasons Change

In Sheffield's heart, where nature gleams,
Meersbrook Park, a place to reflect on dreams.
With every step, life's chaos fades to a blur,
It's nature's peace I happily prefer.

The cities noise, it fades away,
As I find solace in the light of day.
From hectic meetings to that rustling tree,
I breathe deep as my dog runs wild and free.

Autumn leaves begin to fall,
The crunch underfoot enchants us all.
In Spring, daffodils and crocus in bloom,
A burst of hope to end the wintery gloom.

Through every season, the park holds stresses at
bay,
A tranquil refuge, not far away.
No matter when you choose to roam,
Meersbrook Park always feels like home.

A place to wonder, reflect and play,
In Sheffield's heart, where dreams make their
way.

Beyond the Four

Love, happy, mad and sad,
Emotions taught by Mum and Dad.
Four emotions, but life's not so plain,
A rainbow of feelings flows through my vein.

What about jealousy, shame and self-doubt,
What about losing Coldplay tickets to a tout?
Sitting in school, feeling rather glum,
or at Boundary Park, where feet go numb.

Love, happy, mad, and sad,
Life's a blend of good and bad.
Laughter so deep it makes you cry,
Moments you feel like you could touch the sky.

From feeling lost, not quite in command,
To marching through the streets taking a stand.
Sometimes it's joy, sometimes it's a fight,
Through the ups and downs, trust you'll find
your light.

Music

Music fills my ears,
I hum along and forget my fears.
Shuffle is a dangerous move,
Some of these tracks are not my groove.

I tap my ear to skip,
The mood soon begins to dip.
I tap at my ear again,
I'll find the right song, it's just a question of
when.

Sharing my password was a silly mistake,
She says that's an interesting take.
Apparently it's my songs that are the issue,
Depressing, in need of a tissue.

Plinky plonky is not my sound,
Ah, Children, the tune is found.
My thoughts fade away,
And I play the same song again, just to keep
them at bay.

Failures

It's easy to talk about life's wins,
But some weeks I forget to put out the bins.
It's easy to talk about the moments that make
you shine,
Less so about those that make us whine.

I try to be positive and always smile
But some weeks feel like an uphill mile.
I am British so love a moan;
P*ss me off and you'll hear the groan.

Part of being human is to massively fail,
Like walking the dog in shorts, in wind and hail.
I want to challenge myself and expand my brain
So I'll start by writing a sh*t poem, at the back
of a train.

Not your Average Aunties

The adult's path stretches long and wide,
Some pressures mount like a relentless tide.
"Have kids!" is the world's not-so-silent plea,
But for us, that's just not our cup of tea.

As a loving couple, forging our way,
We've chosen a different role to play.
No nappies or sleepless nights to bear,
It's our path, we're happy to declare.

Responsibilities still fill our days,
Life pursuits thrive in numerous ways.
On this journey, we pave our own track,
Defying norms with humour, we don't look
back.

As Aunties, we find joy in the role,
Delight in the little ones, their hearts and soul.
We playfully tussle, making them giddy and
bright,
Tickling them, capturing the perfect moments,
love takes flight.

In our kitchen, biscuits of love we bake,
A sprinkle of laughter, in every bite's wake.
With the hosepipe, they splash and jubilate,
Our affection for them, eternally innate.

So if parenthood is not your call,
Remember it's your life after all.
You define your path, your dreams to chase,
Keep going until you find your content space.

Fireworks

As the fireworks fly in the air,
For the animals we show little care.
Supposed to be one night's flare,
But for a month, the sky they share.

Maybe it's a sign of getting old,
Younger me thought it was gold.
Memories of bonfires burning bright,
Late on a Saturday night.

Now, thoughts shift to our dear Earth,
Fun that damages, we must give it a wide berth.
For the creatures, and the air we breathe,
Time to show the planet some reprieve.

The Future

We dream of the tomorrows, neglecting the now,
Chasing the future, wondering just how.
Can we envision what's never been seen?
Explore the places where we've never been.

Close your eyes, let your imagination soar,
A world uncharted, forever more.
Beyond the known, the familiar scenes,
Embrace the unknown, where possibility
convenes.

Talk of today, weave dreams into now,
Find your path, discover how.
In the unexplored, let your thoughts glean,
The magic of places you've not yet seen.

Packing

I pack my bag, it's only one night
I forgot my charger, it gives me a fright.
Double-checking everything with care,
Wondering just what the f*ck to wear.

Rain or sun, the eternal debate,
A massive case, tempting fate?
Overthinking, I'm in a clutch,
Oh, wait, am I the butch?

It's only 300 miles, I could shop on the way
Emotions leading, making me sway.
Taking all I own, a hefty load,
Can you sense my tone, it's a packing ode.

Not a laughing matter, my brain's a chatter,
Packing drama, emotions, what's the matter?

Trains

All aboard the laughter train, oh joy,
Where seats are rarer than a calm convoy.
Heat like a sauna, a commuter's delight,
Chewing symphonies, an orchestra in flight.

Bags play thrones, on seats they rest,
Shoes join the party, oh, what a jest.
Phones scream for signal, a futile quest,
In the carriage circus, irritation at its best.

WiFi moans and delays in the mix,
Work awaits, lost in a time fix.
Payday dreams, but here comes the fun,
On this train of chaos, everyone's on the run.

Loud conversations, a phone call spree,
In the comedy of chaos, who can it be?
Amidst the laughter, the journey prevails,
A daily sitcom on commuter trails.

Hurkle Durkle

A 200-year-old term rolls of the tongue,
To lounge in bed way too long.

The rain outside lashes down,
Told to get up, I raise a frown.
The issue is, I stayed up late,
Eating too much cheese with my mate.

I need a lazy day,
Staying in bed is my way.
Scrolling through socials, playing sims,
The odd podcast, whatever whims.

So in bed I stay,
It's Sunday, I'll do it my way.
Hurkle,
Durkle.

Coffee Shop Working

Sat in the corner nook,
Enjoying a good book.
Coffee grinding, milk steaming,
Gingerbread biscuits, faces gleaming.

If only inside voices were used,
If you're not bothered, you're the accused.
Your mate is a metre away,
You're shouting like they're in Cayton bay.

Look around, people are trying to chill,
Eyes roll as I reach for a headache pill.
Coffee shop working,
Coffee shop, not working.

The Questions of Adulthood

Why did I want to leave school? Why did I ever want to grow up?

What's for tea? Do we need to go to the shops?
What time do we need to leave? What's the weather like?
Is my train on time? Is my taxi here yet?
When will I be home? What shall we watch?

Did I pack the shopping bags?

…Why do we have a bag

….of bags?

When does my car tax expire? What's it even for?
When did my wardrobe become a collection of 'comfortable' clothes?

Why does the pile of unread books on my shelf
keep growing?
Why do people behave like this? Why do people
behave like that?

When can I sleep for 8 hours? When do I go to
the gym?
When are you free? When am I free?
When did my snack preferences shift from
sweets to nuts and dried fruits?

Some things will never be understood in time.
Some things have no reason, nor rhyme.

The Mist

Energy dwindling, head wrapped in a groggy
haze,
Concentration falters, lost in the foggy maze.
Just an hour, let the mist transcend,
Yet the past lingers, echoes to mend.

Boxes stacked, burdens far from light,
A battlefield unfolds in the sleepless night.
An SAS roll out from the haven of bed,
Yesterday's session dances in the mind's thread.

Coffee's warm embrace, a comforting hold,
A plunge into the lake, in waters cold.
Walking the dog, a bid to clear the head.
Yet the heart yearns to return to bed.

Week by week, combatting the sombre streak,
An hour's skirmish, in an ever-long week.

One sixty-seven more to go,
High, low, high, low, life's ebb and flow.

In the Flow

Whoo hoo my brain is in the flow,
C'mon, email inbox, let's go!
I wade through, ticking off the list,
Even had a break, and the dog's been kissed.

I smile and gleam with delight,

Oh f*ck…

It's 3 o'clock…

….at night.

We Miss You

Silent tears, a mournful sound,
Echoes of loss, an ache so loud.
Embraced by sorrow, a heavy cloak,
Through the pain of loss

…Love spoke.

In the hush of grief, healing starts,
Love's whispers mend broken hearts.
Within the tears, resilience springs,
Nurturing hope

…with tender wings.

Remembering them is always tough,
In time, a smile finds its way through the rough.

The love of a dog

Underneath the open sky,
Walking the woods, furry friend close by.
Through fields and meadows, wildflowers
bloom,
Soon our hearts will surely run out of room.

Eager eyes and a wagging tail,
Cheering us up, never a fail.
Squirrels she chases, running free,
Her company is the happiness key.

Her loyalty, a human's guide,
In every moment, by our side.
In her presence, worries fade,
Furry feet, white teeth, memories are made.

I have a favourite tree

When did I start to look up with glee?
…When the heck did I get a favourite tree?
I once cared less, in youth's fleeting days,
Now I ponder foliage with an affectionate glaze.

Bare branches in a wintry dance,
In Spring, blossoms burst, leaving me in a
trance.
Summer's lush canopy stretches high,
Autumn reveals colours in the crisp, cool sky.

A mighty oak with branches so grand,
A sprightly willow, swaying in the land.
Perhaps the maple, with its fiery attire,
In my tree-ranking quest, I won't tire.

I scoffed at those who'd declare,
A tree they loved, with an affectionate air.
Yet here I stand, guilty as can be,
Save the trees, I shout in plea!

So here's to the leafy, the barky, the grand,
To the one that stands out in this wooded land.
I laugh at myself, oh, can't you see,
When the heck did I get a favourite tree?

www.ingramcontent.com/pod-product-compliance
Lightning Source LLC
LaVergne TN
LVHW050934200726